The Polish Immigrant and His Reading

by

Eleanor E. Ledbetter

Librarian, Broadway Branch
Cleveland Public Library
Chairman, A.L.A. Committee on
Work with the Foreign Born

Chicago   American Library Association   1924

CONTENTS

Foreword 3

The Polish immigrant and his reading.. 5

  The church 8

  The parochial school 9

  The Polish press 11

  The Polish temperament 12

  The first visit to the library 14

  What shall he read?.. 16

  Polish literature.. 17

  Publishers, editions and methods of purchase. 20

  American publishers and dealers 21

  Periodicals and newspapers.. 22

  The second generation 22

Suggested list of titles for a beginning collection in the Polish
  language 24

  Fiction 24

  Language 33

  Song books 33

  Biography . . . 33

  Domestic science 34

  United States history, civics, etc 34

  Polish history 35

  Travel 35

  Literature 36

  Translations from other literatures 37

FOREWORD

Complete community service is the goal of the progressive public library—a book for every man, a book that he can use, the right book at the right time. To choose the right books and to get them into the hands of the right persons is a task which can be successfully accomplished only by the librarian who has an understanding of the community, its actual and its possible reading interests.

When the community contains many foreign born, the need for understanding is especially urgent. Each immigrant race has its own characteristics, intellectual and social, which make it individual. The degree of education in the Old World affects the amount of library use possible in the New. The character of employment determines the amount of leisure available for reading. The social organization may be a barrier or an aid, according to the method of approach.

In almost all cases it is desirable to add to the library books in the native tongue of local groups. Some can never learn to read English with ease and all enjoy best the type of story characteristic of their native literature, just as most men remain always faithful to "mother's cooking." It has been customary for libraries to buy books in French, German, Spanish and Italian for readers studying those languages for the cultural value. It is just as important to preserve in the immigrant the cultural values of Czech, Polish, Roumanian, Lithuanian and other literatures. Each has its distinctive merits and its characteristic spiritual quality.

The geographical situation which has been so great a factor in our development as a nation has kept us from those contacts with other people's languages and literatures which are an integral part of the education of a European scholar. Consequently our ignorance is very great; and our difficulty as librarians dealing with the foreign born lies in the fact that we know the people so little and their literatures scarcely at all.

This series of pamphlets is therefore prepared by the Committee on Work with the Foreign Born to furnish guidance, help and understanding. It is designed in each pamphlet to set forth those characteristics of a racial group which influence its receptiveness to library activities,—its possibilities and its limitations in the way of books and reading; to show what means have been found most effective in establishing contacts with its members; and to give general information about their literatures, with definite suggestions regarding choice of titles and methods of purchase.

The Polish immigrant and the library is the first publication in the series. The Poles are an important immigrant group of distinct character with a rich and varied literature, to which this pamphlet furnishes only the briefest of introductions. Additional information may be found in the following articles in the magazine *Poland:*

Polish literature, by Clarence A. Manning, in March 1924.
Poland's literary revival, by Charles Phillips, in February and March 1924.
Polish literature in English, by Eleanor E. Ledbetter, in April 1924.

The Oxford University Press has just published two important volumes, *Periods of Polish literary history* and *Modern Polish literature* by Roman Dyboski, professor of English in the University of Cracow and lecturer at King's College and at Oxford University.

ELEANOR E. LEDBETTER,
Chairman, Committee on Work with the Foreign Born.

A POLISH VILLAGE

Typical of those from which our immigrants come.

THE POLISH IMMIGRANT AND
HIS READING

To Americans the Poles are the best known of the Slavic
group. Their independent history is most recent. All stu-
dents know the crime of the partition of Poland. Kosciusko
and Pulaski fighting with us and for us in our revolution
established for their nation a permanent claim upon our interest and sympathy. Every American has a mental picture
of how "Freedom shrieked when Kosciusko fell," although
he mispronounces the hero's name. The information of the
average American stops right here, but the person who
really wishes to make friends with the Polish people must
know much more. The librarian who would contribute to
their culture and education through the medium of the public
library must have a fairly detailed understanding of their
past, of their national character, and of the conditions of the
European situation which preceded their emigration.

A foundation for this understanding may be secured
through the librarian's own medium, the printed page. *Poland, the knight among nations,* by Van Norman, is the best
single book, and gives a certain amount of both history and
interpretation. *A brief history of Poland,* by Julia Swift
Orvis, is very readable, and *Poland,* by Phillips, in the Home
University Library, is a good brief volume, especially strong
on modern conditions. *The litany of the Polish pilgrim,*
by Mickiewicz, greatest of Polish poets, concentrates in a
few words the essence of Polish history, religion, and national feeling, and its petitions now seem to have been
prophetic. This splendid bit of literature is conveniently
found in Monica M. Gardner's *Life of Adam Mickiewicz.*

The Polish Information Committee of London has published a number of pamphlets on such topics as *Landmarks of Polish history* and *The national music of Poland,* which give excellent information in brief and convenient form.

A background of knowledge thus secured, one should become absorbed in the national feeling through the medium of the great trilogy of Sienkiewicz, *With fire and sword, The deluge,* and *Pan Michael.* One whose spirit has kindled with Kmita's in his prodigious deeds of valor during the Swedish siege of the shrine of Czenstohowa, will see in every American Polish church a reflection of Czenstohowa, and in every Polish priest a suggestion of the indomitable prior Kordecki.

The mentality of the peasant is interpreted in some of the short stories of Sienkiewicz; *Sielanka* is a beautiful picture of country life; *Bartek the Victor,* a painful true delineation of the bewilderment of the peasant under a foreign military dominance; and *For bread* portrays the sufferings of some early immigrants to America. These three stories may be found in various collections of the minor writings of Sienkiewicz.

Then in order to balance the picture by a realization that the Pole's self-interpretation is not the interpretation of his neighbors, one should read Gogol's great work *Taras Bulba,* and try to realize that the Ukrainian nationalist in America hates the Polish nation just as Bulba did, although unlike Bulba, he may be friendly to individual Poles. "The oppression psychosis and the immigrant," by Herbert Adolphus Miller, in the *Annals of the American Academy,* January, 1921, must not be omitted, since it gives the key to mental attitudes otherwise difficult to understand.

Finally one must know that the Poles of America are politically divided into parties between whom no bridge exists ; and that the acquaintance of each party must be sought as separately as that of Ulsterites and Sinn Fein. One party is identified with the Polish National Alliance and the Polish Roman Catholic Union, the other with the National Defense Committee (known by the Polish initials K.O.N.) ; both are working for the development and upbuilding of the new Poland, but without co-operation. The K. O. N. party is accused of being anti-clerical and socialistic, and some of its leaders are outspoken foes of the parochial school; while the National Alliance members are in general conservative and conformists.

Policy and good feeling suggest also the wisdom of at least an elementary acquaintance with Polish phonetics. The correct pronunciation of a foreign name is a sort of high sign proving that one belongs to the initiate. It is true that Polish names do look formidable, the preponderance of z's being especially staggering. But the formidableness is in appearance only; *sz* is just as good a combination of letters as *sh, cz* as *ch,* when one knows that they represent the same sound. Every letter always has the same sound and is always sounded. One has only to start at the beginning of a name and keep going, accenting the penult when he gets to it. The necessary simple rules may be found in many places, such as the appendix to *With fire and sword,* the preface to *The deluge,* the appendix to Van Norman's *Poland;* while the librarian who wishes a little technical knowledge of the language may secure it through Baluta's *Practical handbook of the Polish language,* published by the Polish Book Importing Company in New York.

Acquaintance must be initiated along lines of natural contact. The librarian should absorb all she can from every Pole whom she meets, asking questions as an interested friend, not as a professional investigator. A walk through the district is always illuminating to a good observer, and one can drop into a corner grocery to inquire one's way, and linger to converse a while, extending an invitation to the library as a return courtesy. Such informal excursions are absolutely essential to a visualization of neighborhood conditions as related to the possible use of books and the library, and they should form a part of the librarian's regular routine.

"The quiet work of air and moisture" was a chapter heading in an old geology. The gist of its theme was that the quiet work of air and moisture, going on unremittingly day in and day out, summer and winter, has wrought far greater changes in the earth's surface than all the earthquakes, all the avalanches, all the tidal waves and all the volcanic eruptions that have ever taken place. So in any work with immigrant people, the quiet work of personal interest and friendly assistance will accomplish more than all the brass bands and all the mass meetings ever staged—although the brass band and the mass meeting have their mission too.

And the librarian, working as unremittingly as do the air and moisture in the quiet work of personal contacts, will also seek for mass movements through the formal agencies of the church, the press, and the school.

The Church

Almost all Poles are faithful Roman Catholics, giving as a rule unquestioned obedience to the advice of their pastors. The librarian must therefore put no limit to her efforts to win for the library the active approval and recommendation of the local priest. The method must always be individual, depending on the idiosyncrasies of the local situation and on the personality of the priest and of the librarian. There is no advantage in trying to make the acquaintance on the ground of a common faith. A Roman Catholic is more easily turned down by an unfriendly priest than is a Protestant, who, not recognizing authority in him, feels no inhibition to keep her from persistence. The foreign born Polish clergy who have not already had acquaintance with a public library are apt to have very erroneous ideas regarding its character and functions, imagining that its books are all either frivolous or materialistic. The best way to convert such a one is of course to get him to the library and to show him its contents and methods; if that cannot be done, then books or book lists must be taken to him, choosing themes with which he is familiar, so that he can personally weigh their value. Here again the quiet work of sincere friendly interest is bound to produce an ultimate response, which will probably come in the opportunity to do him a personal favor. When that time comes the favor should be done, regardless of time or trouble.

Tact and diplomacy are sometimes needed also where the parish considers itself provided for by a library of its own. The public library must then be demonstrated as supplementing the parish collection with greater resources and a wider range of themes. As the parish collection is expensive to maintain and troublesome to administer, there is always a possibility that after a while it may be turned over to the public library. During the war some such collections were sent to the Polish army, because their owners, using the public library, no longer needed them.

The Parochial School

Next to the church is the parochial school, which most Polish children attend. Courtesy requires the priest's permission before visiting the school, where the Sister Superior must first be sought. The principal orders teaching in Polish

parochial schools are: The Sisters of the Holy Family of
Nazareth; The Felician Sisters; the Franciscan Sisters of
St. Kunegunda; the Sisters of the Resurrection; and the
Polish Sisters of St. Joseph. These Sisters have under their
care considerably more than one hundred thousand children.
The Sisters of St. Joseph, although a comparatively small
order, teach 21,660 pupils.

All these orders are made up of women of Polish parentage, most of whom have themselves been educated in parochial schools in this country. A large proportion entered the
convent directly from the grammar grades, completing their
education in the academy of the order during their novitiate.
Thus very few of them had any acquaintance with public libraries before beginning their teaching, and the librarian
must win her way in the school by first making the library
valuable to the teachers. The cloistered life is literally and
actually a life shut away from the world and without knowledge of the world; therefore all the advances must come
from the library side. The Sister cannot ask for aids of
which she has never heard; the librarian must offer her
wares and demonstrate their usefulness.

A golden opportunity for service is at hand in the fact
that many Sisters in these orders are now studying diligently
and systematically through summer schools, correspondence
courses, and extension classes toward a goal of recognized
standard credentials. The librarian can render an inestim-
able service to the cause of education and a friendly service
great in personal reward by connecting these teachers with
local educational advantages, the availability of which they
do not know. Nowhere will she find gratitude more touch-
ing, friendship more complete than that which follows such
a service. A religious community is a big family and service
to one part of the family influences the whole group. Good

library service in Menasha, Wisconsin, produces results in Cleveland, Ohio, or Pittsburgh, Pennsylvania, and the news of what libraries can do spreads, not only from Sister to Sister, but from order to order.

Acquaintance with school and teachers brings invitations to school entertainments in the parish hall, where one may meet parents and friends. This leads naturally to attendance at the musical and dramatic entertainments given by the various parish organizations. Public friendly attention by the priest gives standing and inspires confidence and an invitation to sit upon the platform must be regarded as official recognition of one's work.

In the average Polish settlement, most social activities are in connection with the church, just as they are in American villages; but in large city colonies there are also independent societies, such as chapters of the Veterans of the Polish Army and musical and dramatic organizations, whose friendship is worth cultivating.

The Polish Press

The church, the school, and the press are the three universal agencies to be enlisted in work with the foreign born. The Polish press, like every other press, has two fundamental intentions; first, to give its readers what they are interested in, and second, to give them what the editor wants them to be interested in. The amount of space which the library may expect depends upon its balance between these two considerations. Before planning newspaper publicity the librarian should examine the newspapers she wishes to use, studying their arrangement and division of space; how much is foreign news, how much official society business, and how much local news, and the relative appearance and prominence of each. Even though she does not know Polish she can observe with sufficient intelligence for this purpose, and can thus know how to gauge the publicity she may receive. The long essaylike article giving a general account of the whole library has no place in the foreign language press. An article of not more than one hundred and fifty words developing simply and clearly a single idea is the one which will produce the best results. A whole column is the tribute which a newspaper may give once to a fine monument; a succession of short items is news of a live institution. These items may be prepared in English and offered to the editor as suggestions merely. He will then, according to his mood, either translate them literally or use them as texts for themes of his own composition. This co-operation may be confidently expected, but the librarian must be prepared also for the fact that every Polish editor is victim to some degree of the oppression psychosis and is likely to break out in the most unexpected place. A Polish paper, for instance, commented scathingly on the absence of Polish assistants in its local library, and at the same time the editor admitted privately that he did not know a single qualified person available for recommendation. One has to learn not to take these things too seriously. After all, criticism indicates interest; to be ignored is worse.

The Polish Temperament

The average Polish immigrant is timid and shy. In the Old World he occupied an inferior position and was always made to feel his inferiority; he never traveled and he knew little except his immediate surroundings. The enormous wrench of coming to America temporarily exhausts his initiative and demands the relaxation of settling down in the Polish colony where he seeks to have things as much like home as possible. From this relaxation he emerges slowly to an acquaintance with American institutions. Shyness and humility are qualities which have in them elements of loveliness; masked by a protective covering of apparent indifference or hostility they fail of their true appraisal. The librarian must see through the mask and provide ease for the shyness, equality for the humility.

To do this it is essential that the library atmosphere be one of friendly hospitality and sympathetic interest. An easy informality of entrance should be provided for even in the architectural design, and must be supplemented by a socially minded staff trained to gracious manners, quick observation, and keen analysis. Such a staff intuitively recognizes Timid Stranger's first visit and invites him in if his courage threatens to fail him in the vestibule. The necessary registration questions, prefaced by a "Good morning" or "Good evening," will be carefully phrased; never a blunt "How do you spell it?" because Poles are not accustomed to spelling by letter; rather, "Will you write it, please?" And if he says "Good-bye" on leaving he will be answered as though that courtesy were our own custom.

Such a policy consistently carried on will eventuate in some visitor's saying, in a burst of unrestraint, "The Polish people like very much the way they are treated at the library," and the speaker will never know that in those words the librarian feels the laurel crown upon her brow. Scarcely twice in a lifetime can one hope for such a tribute as came from an educated foreign social worker who spoke with tears in his eyes of a group of librarians, saying, "I thought to myself, these are American *intelligentsia,* and they are *intelligentsia,* not only of the mind, but of the soul."

The First Visit to the Library

Because the Polish immigrant is shy and timid, the easiest way to introduce him to the library is in a group of his own sort. The most ideal introduction is that of a night school class brought by an interested teacher who permits his name to be used as reference in the library registration and who assists in the first choice of books. In Cleveland this was done voluntarily for years by interested teachers who gave up a free evening for the purpose; later the Board of Education, convinced of its value, gave permission for one regular evening of each term to be so spent. The teacher's signature must be used for reference and identification only, as it is obvious that he cannot assume financial responsibility for all his pupils. The risk involved is slight, as night school classes are made up for the most part of serious and responsible men, anxious for advancement and sensible of obligation. The library rules should be explained in Polish in order to make sure of complete understanding, red tape should be reduced to a minimum and the rules so adjusted that books may be drawn that very evening. The chances are that every member of the class will take an English book for study and a Polish book for recreational reading, and that a large proportion of the class will come regularly on the same evening of the week for months following.

The same method of group visiting and group registration may be carried through with sodality, lodge, or other organization; but it is essential to secure preliminary assurance of leadership from some member who has used the library and who is willing to put his personal influence and some effort into rounding up the crowd for the visit. A written invitation from the librarian, presented formally at a regular meeting of the organization and there accepted formally, is a suitable and proper preliminary, and makes a better impression upon Polish susceptibilities than an informal, "Get your society to come." The natural dignity of the Polish character demands a certain formality of approach, and deficiency in that respect is often a cause of lack of response.

A Polish man who had grown up without educational opportunity was thoroughly imbued with the idea of natural inferiority. In his own words, "I always thought I was a dumbhead." Drawn as experimental material into a demonstration class in the factory, it came to him as a great revelation that he too could learn. The whole world assumed a new aspect. He became a man instead of a creature. Working twelve hours a day, feeding a furnace which was "always hungry," on night shift alternate two weeks so that no regular classes were available to him, he engaged a private teacher who met him at the library and with whom he studied with the greatest diligence. His ambition grew by leaps and bounds and soon he engaged also a Polish teacher in order that he might be able to write back to the Old Country of the wonderful development which had come to him here— which was, after all, only that he had learned that he was as good as anyone else. We are apt to think of democracy as a leveling down process. To be a good democrat means to meet as equals persons whom we might consider as beneath us; to the average immigrant it is a leveling up process; he has to learn to regard himself as the equal of those whom he naturally would have regarded as his superiors. Until this sense of democracy is established, formality has a part to play. Informality is understood only between those who recognize each other as equals. But the formal invitation must not be relied upon to do all the work. It must be preceded by personal conversations with individuals who are interested, preferably with officers of the society, who will speak favorably when it is presented. Then when the group come, let them be received hospitably and given every possible attention. A special order of the day should sweep aside as far as possible all other work and free the library assistants for full attention to the new visitors. The regular public will be interested and will waive most of their own claims for the evening.

What Shall He Read?

Such a visit may be arranged by any library as an exhibition of a civic institution and for this alone it is worth while; but it will not produce an appreciable increase of library circulation unless the library contains Polish books. These are needed by the Poles for the same reason that all immigrants need books in their own languages, namely for recreational reading and for the fuller understanding of informational reading which is possible only where one comprehends every shade of meaning. For the Poles an additional most potent reason lies in the seemingly irrelevant fact that Germany and Russia designed the suppression of the Polish language. In Russian Poland Russian was the medium of instruction in the schools, and fines were imposed on any person guilty of teaching reading and writing without official authority—which meant, of course, guilty of teaching Polish; while in Poznan (German Poland) Polish was forbidden not only in the schools but even as a medium of religious instruction. (See W. A. Phillips, *Poland*, pp. 166, 167, 196, 201ff.) Because the prohibited thing becomes by the very fact of prohibition eminently desirable these German and Russian prohibitions increased to the point of fanaticism the devotion of the Poles to their own tongue. A textbook of English *Przewodnik polsko-angielski,* by Maryanski, shows the complex which has resulted from this attempted suppression in the following sentences in the introductory lesson:

"I am a Pole and I strongly desire that my children remain the same."

"I desire that my children may learn the English, but in the first place they must learn the Polish language, the language of my fathers and forefathers."

"Poland is your mother whom you ought to honor and love with heart and soul."

"By all means do not forget that you are a Pole and be proud of being a son of a country which was the emblem of heroism and freedom."

One need not be a psychoanalyst to see that the only way to overcome this feeling is to remove all opposition; to show the Pole that we respect his language, admire his literature, and regard sympathetically his devotion to it. The material advantage of English to himself and his children is so great that one need not fear an exclusive devotion to Polish beyond the time when generous treatment has removed this old world psychosis.

Polish Literature

Polish literature, moreover, merits a place with other cultural literatures. Sienkiewicz may be read in the original to as great advantage as Coulevain or Galdós; and in Polish as in French and Spanish there is a volume of literature of superior quality which has never been translated into English and which is lost to our culture but still available to the Pole. The *Tales from the Polish* and *More tales from the Polish,* by Elsie M. Benecke, and the Polish selections in Selver's *Anthology of modern Slavonic literatures* give tantalizing glimpses of the character and quality of this literary

field so little known. The Polish writer is a master of the
word picture and in this art he has no match in American
literature. Characteristic Polish fiction is largely historical
and based upon the national history. Sienkiewicz is known
to us in translation. Kraszewski is also a master of historical narrative, and wrote voluminously. *Quo vadis,* which
introduced Sienkiewicz to the English reading public, is by
Poles much less esteemed than his national romances. Un-
doubtedly the first Polish books for a library are the favorite
trilogy *Ogniem i mieczem (With fire and sword), Potop
(The deluge)* ; and *Pan Wolodyowski (Pan Michael). Na
polu chwaly (On the field of glory), Krzyzacy (The knights
of the cross),* and the short stories of the master may well
come next; then a selection from Kraszewski: *Jaszko Or-
fanem, Krzyzacy, Pogrobek* are desirable, but any of his
works are acceptable. Next I would choose some romances
from Rodziewicowna and Orzeskowa, since these appeal especially to women. *Dewajtis,* generally considered the best
work of the former, is one of the most popular books in the
library. The heroine, having spent most of her childhood
in America, returns to Poland as a young woman, and the
romance links the two countries together, and presents a
picture of immigrant life. Other very popular authors of
fiction are:

Dmochowska	Konopnicka
Gasiorowski	Mniszek
Gawalewicz	Przyborowski
Glowacki	Reymont
Gomulicki	Walewski
Gruszecki	Zeromski

Pseudonyms are greatly used; J. J. Jez is the pen-name of
Zygmunt Milkowski; Boleslaw Prus of Alexander Glowacki.
Confusion is avoided by cataloging uniformly under the real

name, which may be learned from *Pseudonimy i kryptonimy polskie,* by Ludwig Czarkowski.

Sienkiewicz, Kraszewski, and Glowacki should form the backbone of a Polish fiction collection. Their works are for the most part based on events in Polish history, often giving the best available picture of a given period. Reymont's *Chlopi (The peasants)* is also a book of the first importance. Writers of the post-war period also use the historical setting, but the setting with which they are personally familiar, as for example Bandrowski, who writes novels of Russian conditions, and Malaczewski, whose *Horse on the hill* is a collection of sketches based on scenes actually witnessed. His death, at the age of 26, was a loss to Polish letters, and was the result of sufferings he had endured.

In many of the modern writers there is a strong over-emphasis on the subject of sex, sufficient to make careful selection necessary, even in the choice of titles of such an author as Zeromski. His literary rank is of the highest and some of his books have exerted very great influence in the development of Polish thought, but there are others which are not desirable for general use in public libraries.

The *Bible* is much called for, and will find use in even a small Polish collection. Dyniewicz's *History of the United States* is a text by a Polish author; Pecorini's *Historia Ameryki* is available with Polish and English in parallel texts. A good history of Poland is by Lewinski, another by Limanowski; Van Norman's *Poland, the knight among nations,* has been translated into Polish. The *History of Polish literature* by Chmielowski is recommended. The Pole is very fond of reading books of travel, and will use all the interesting books that can be furnished along that line, but of course there has been no traveling for years, and consequently no new books. Lives of saints are always in demand, and the collection by Skarga *Zywoty Swietych* is a popular addition to the library. Formerly an excellent edition in two volumes was available; one not so satisfactory is in twelve small volumes. *Winiec liliowy (The wreath of lilies)* by Podbielski is also a religious book of great appeal

Polish literature is rich in the cultural classes—poetry, essays, the drama; and the average Pole reads these more than the average American does works of the same quality; but the average immigrant does most of his reading for recreation and relaxation, and like his American brother wishes for this purpose a large proportion of fiction and romance.

Publishers, Editions, and Methods of Purchase

At the present time the purchase of a select list of Polish books is accomplished with some difficulty, but conditions are rapidly improving. During the war there was great destruction in Poland both of books and of facilities for printing. When the Polish republic was established, a first essential was the publication of school books, as public education in the Polish language only then came into existence. This need provided for, a great volume of new literature clamored for expression and distribution, and many new authors have come to the front. At present there is a definite program for republishing the old standards, many of which had been exhausted during the war. Editions are generally small, and books may become "out of print" in a very short time, and come back again in a few weeks or months. Indication is given on the appended list of titles which were definitely known to be out of print in July, 1923, but which are certain, as standard works, to be reprinted. Before the war, every important Polish publisher took pride in issuing each year two or three beautiful books, often monographs on art subjects, written by authorities and beautifully printed and illustrated. This was in a sense his contribution to arts and letters, and he was satisfied if the edition paid for itself in the course of several years. Now this is impossible. The publisher cannot afford to publish anything on which he will not get his return within a year, and the book business is practically on a cash basis. It is, however, possible for American libraries to make arrangements to pay on receipt of goods, the payment being based, as is only fair, on the value of the Polish mark at the time the books were billed.

The largest book business of Poland is that of Gebethner and Wolff, publishers and dealers, with branches in every important Polish city. The main office is Zgoda 12, Warsaw. The firm of M. Arct, Novy Swiat 41, Warsaw, is also recommended. Mr. Stanislaus Arct was formerly Polish High Commissioner to the United States, knows English perfectly, understands the American library's point of view, and gives personal attention to American correspondence.

American Publishers and Dealers

The Polish Book Importing Company, 83 Second Ave., New York, has for years represented all the Polish publishers; the Polish News Agency, 38 Union Square, has a good stock; firms devoted to the general foreign book trade handle Polish of course with the rest. Polish books have been published in America by several firms, of which the most important are Paryzki, 1140 Nebraska Ave., Toledo, and the Polish American Publishing Company, successors to Dyniewicz, 1516 Tell Place, Chicago. They have issued many excellent titles, but unfortunately have used a grade of paper and binding so poor that their books were practically useless for library purposes. The Chicago firm is making a special effort at improvement in this respect.

It is of course more convenient to buy from an American dealer, but there is no difficulty involved in ordering directly from Warsaw. Books are now sent in packages not over 2 kilograms in weight by book post, and the cost is small and service excellent.

Periodicals and Newspapers

The library ought to have Polish periodicals as well as books, and the character and make-up of Polish magazines will be very interesting to the American as well as to the Polish reader. *Tygodnik Illustrowany,* published weekly by Gebethner and Wolff, Zgoda 12, Warsaw, at the present price of nine dollars a year, is an excellent illustrated weekly devoted to art and to current events and is well worth a subscription, though not yet equal in appearance to its before-the-war style. Another desirable periodical is *Swiat,* published at Szpitalna 12, Warsaw, at about the same price. Some libraries could use a Warsaw daily for the fuller news it would bring. *Kurjer Warszawski* is recommended and can be ordered through Paluszek Brothers, Aeolian Building, New York.

The *American newspaper annual* lists seventeen daily, forty-eight weekly and four monthly American publications in the Polish language. Many of their editors are very generous and will donate their papers to public libraries frequented by their people; in other cases the library may well pay for subscriptions in order to provide reading matter for possible patrons who otherwise get no return for their library tax. To develop the habit of coming to the library is an object worthy in itself.

The Second Generation

Because of the indelibleness of the impression left by language oppression, because also of the identification of language, nationality, and religion, the Polish child reads Polish longer than the child of any other race does the language of his immigrant parents; but at that, the second generation reverses the relationship of the languages in his reading. The immigrant reads English for education and information, Polish for relaxation and recreation; his child, on the contrary, reads English for relaxation and recreation, and Polish for culture and for its associations. Thus the Polish books in the library help to prevent the existence of the chasm which in other races too often develops between the immigrant parents and their American children.

Both generations and many Americans also will be interested in the monthly magazine *Poland,* published in the English language at 953 Third Avenue, New York, at $2.00 a year. This magazine is delightfully illustrated and contains authoritative articles on every phase of Polish life, literature, and art as well as trade and industry. Several excellent articles on Polish literature have made the 1923 volume of special value to librarians, and the editorial plans include occasional resumes of new books.

SUGGESTED LIST OF TITLES
FOR A BEGINNING COLLECTION
IN THE POLISH LANGUAGE

The titles in this list have been chosen from those most popular during a period of years in the Cleveland Public Library and from newer titles recommended by competent literary advisers and examined in Warsaw in the summer of 1923. The list thus compiled has been critically reviewed by His Excellency Dr. Wladyslaw Wroblewski, Minister of Poland to the United States, who authorizes a statement of his approval.

Books of fiction suggested as first choice for a very small collection are marked with an asterisk but in the non-fiction list it was thought that librarians would prefer to make their own selection.

Biblia. (The Bible.)

Fiction

Bałucki, Michał. Biały murzyn. (White slave.)
A tale of student life.

——— Błyszczące nędze. (Glittering poverty.)
His novels are characterized by humorous descriptions of Polish high life among the nobility and upper classes, 50 years ago.

Choynowski, Piotr. Kij w mrowisku. (The stick in the ant hill.)

——— Kuźnia. (The blacksmith's shop.)
Poland, just before the rebellion of 1863.

——— Pokusa. (Temptation.)
Short stories, sketches of life.
His works are good in general.

Dąbrowski, Ignacy. Matki. (Mothers.)

——— Samotna. (The lonely one.)

24

Dmochowska, Emma Jelenska. Panienka. (The young lady.)

Gąsiorowski, Wacław. Pani Walewska. (Mrs. Walewska.)
Napoleonic period; good.

*————— Emilia Plater. (Emily Plater.)
A historical novel of Emilia Plater, one of the great heroines of Polish history.
All the books of this author are good.

Gawalewicz, Maryan. Bluszcz. (The ivy leaf.)

————— Dla ziemi. (For our land.)

————— Mechesy.
Story of Jews who turn Christian for the sake of getting up in the social scale.

*Głowacki, Alexander (pseud. Bolesław Prus). Faraon. (Pharaoh.)
A Polish classic, the first choice of Głowacki's works. A story of ancient Egypt, an eclipse of the sun being presented by priests of Isis as their own work, thus completing the subjection of the people.

*————— Lalka. (The doll.)
Picture of life and manners among the nobility awakening to the futility of a life of luxury and to a desire for real usefulness.

————— Emancypantka. (An emancipated woman.)
A woman's demonstration of independence, thirty or forty years ago.

*————— Placowka. (The outpost.)
Story of a Polish peasant family, living near the German border and holding out for Poland, defending their poor sterile farm to the last ditch to keep it from falling into the hands of Germans.

*————— Anielka. (Annie.)
"A beautiful story."

———— Dziwni ludzie. (Some queer people.)

Short stories.
Only the first two of these titles are now in print, but when available others should be added, as Głowacki, Sienkiewicz, and Kraszewski should furnish the backbone of any Polish collection.

Gomulicki, Wiktor. Car widmo. (The vision of the tsar.)

Gruszecki, Artur. W tysiąc lat. (In a thousand years.)

———— Dla miliona. (For a million.)

———— Krety. (The moles.)

A story of life among the Polish miners.
A popular writer, whose works all have a good purpose though not of great literary value.

Jeske-Choinski, Teodor. Gasnace słońce. (Dying sun.)

A fantastic story of a time in the future when the sun begins to cool, salvation coming in the collision of the sun with another star, the heat of collision restoring the earth again.

Konopnicka, Marya. Pod prawem. (Under the law.)

———— Z przeszłości. (From the past.)

*———— Ludzie. (The people.)

Korczak, Janusz. Krol Maciuś pierwszy. (King Matthew the first.)

———— Krol Maciuś na wyspie bezludnej. (King Matthew on a desert island.)

These books will be enjoyed by children as well as adults.

———— Sława. (Glory.)

*****Kraszewski, Józef.** Stara basn. (Tale of olden times.)

By many considered Kraszewski's best. A story of the earliest national development in Lithuania.

*———— Krzyżacy. (Knights of the cross.)
Similar theme to Sienkiewicz's book of the same title.

*———— Pogrobek. (The orphaned prince.)

———— Bajbuza.

———— Jelita.
Historical novel of the period of Ladisław Lokietek.

———— Lubonie. (The Lubons.)
Setting is the early period of Polish history, the time of Bolesław the Great.

———— Przygody Pana Marka Hinzy. (The adventures of Mr. Markus Hinz.)
Humorous narrative.

*———— Syn Jazdona. (Son of Jazdon.)

———— Stach z Konar. (Stanley from Konar.)
A voluminous writer, whose works all have a Polish historical setting. With Sienkiewicz and Głowacki should be largely represented.

Krechowiecki, Adam. Fiat lux. (Let there be light.)

———— Veto! (Veto!)
A very good author.

Ligocki, Edward. Sen o Dwernickim. (A dream about Dvernicki.)
Story built around the character and life of Dvernicki, who was a Polish general in the revolutionary attempt of 1830.

———— Płonące Reims. (Reims in flames.)
A novel of the world war.

———— Sambra i Moza. (Sambre and Meuse.)
On the battlefields in France.
A contemporary writer of excellent standing.

Łozinski, Władysław. Madonna Busowiska. (The Busowisk Madonna.)

Life in a Polish village; very beautiful.

———— Oko proroka. (The eye of the prophet.)

Charming story of the experiences of a little boy seeking his father who had been carried away prisoner by the Turks. The child wins friends and secures his father's release.

Maciejowski, Ignacy (pseud. Sewer). Matka. (Mother.)

A peasant mother educates her son at the expense of much sacrifice.

———— Jabłko szatana. (Apple of Satan.)

Makuszynski, Kornel. Perły i wieprze. (Pearls and pigs.)

Humorous tales.

———— Po mlecznej drodze. (Along the milky way.)

Story of artist life in Poland.

———— Słonće w herbie. (The sun in the coat of arms.)

Petty noble, veteran of 1863, keeps number of his comrades in his household; educates his son in Paris. Father dies, son returns and drives out the old friends except one who has a lovely daughter. The young man falls in love and under her influence seeks out and recalls the old men.

Małaczewski, Eugeniusz. Koń na wzgorzu. (The horse on the hill.)

One of the most important post-war books, descriptive of the conflict between the Poles and the Bolsheviks; written with great talent and high moral tone.

Morawska, Zuzanna. Na posterunku. (At the post.)

———— Na dworze krolowej Anny. (At the court of Queen Anne.)

Very good light fiction.

Mniszek, Helen (pseud. Radomyska). Trędowata. (The victim of caste.)

Story of a young lord of exalted position and family, who loves a beautiful and lovely girl of rank lower than his own.

A very popular book.

———— Ordynat Michorowski. (Michorowski's heir.)
Sequel to "Trędowata."

———— Verte. (Turn about.)
A very popular author, of no literary value, but pleasing and greatly liked by women.

*Orzeszkowa, Eliza. Nad Niemnem. (On the Niemen.)

*———— Pan Graba. (Mr. Graba.)

———— Czciciel potęgi. (The worshipper of power.)
A prominent woman writer, always a champion of progressive thought.

Przyborowski, Walery. Chamska dusza. (The common soul.)

———— Męty. (The mire.)

Przerwa-Tetmajer, Kazimierz. Anioł-smierci. (Angel of death.)

———— Panna Mery. (Miss Mary.)

*———— Ze skalnego podhala.
Short stories from the life of mountaineers in Polish Tatra, of highest artistic value.

*Reymont, W. S. Chłopi. (The peasants.)
A classic.

———— Ziemia obiecana. (Promised land.)
Story based on a vision of Poland regained.

———— Fermenty.
A new edition of Reymont is in course of publication.
Under the German occupation, German officers were compelled to read Reymont to acquaint themselves with the psychology of the people they were governing.

*Rodziewiczowną, Marya. Dewajtis.
Story of an American girl of Polish parentage who returns to Poland to take possession of an inheritance. An extremely popular book, generally considered the author's best.

*———— Klejnot. (The jewel.)

———— Straszny dziadzunio. (Stern grandfather.)

———— Z głuszy. (In the wilderness.)

A new edition of Rodziewiczowną's works is in course of publication. They are liked by all readers, but are especially popular with women.

*Sienkiewicz, Henryk. Ogniem i mieczem. (With fire and sword.)

*———— Potop. (The deluge.)

*———— Pan Wołodyowski. (Pan Michael.)

*———— Na polu chwały. (On the field of glory.)

*———— Krzyżacy. (Knights of the cross.)

*———— W pustyni i puszczy. (In desert and wilderness.)

———— Quo vadis.

———— Rodzina połanieckich. (Children of the soil.)

———— Selim Mirza.

———— Przez stepy i inne powieści. (Through the plains and other tales.)

A new edition of Sienkiewicz will be completed by 1925.

*Sieroszewski, Wacław. Beniowski. (Mr. Beniowski.)

A Polish nobleman, exiled by Catherine II, organizes a revolt among his fellow prisoners in Kamchatka. They escape, get possession of a ship and eventually settle in Madagascar where the leader is chosen king by the natives

———— Brzask. (The dawn.)

Short stories.

———— Jesienia. (In autumn.)

Short stories.

———— Małżenstwo. (A married couple.)

———— Ridztau. (A mountain of the Himalayas.)
A story of some political exiles living there.

*———— Z fali na fali. (From wave to wave.)
Short stories.
A modern author of great literary merit; his works are recommended without reservation. He spent many years as an exile in Siberia, where he was sent when only sixteen years old. First recognition came for his work as an ethnologist.

Stasiak, Ludwik. Brandenburg. (Brandenburg.)

———— Obrona sztandaru. (Defense of the colors.)

Strug, Andrzej. Ojcowie nasi. (Our fathers.)

———— Pieniądz. (Money.)

———— Portret. (A portrait.)
A prominent worker for national independence; early writings socialistic in tone, later ones not. All are stories of contemporary life.

Walewska, M. J. Pani El. (Mrs. El.)

Wasylewski, Stanisław. Księżna Pani. (Madam princess.)

———— Na dworze krolewskim. (At the royal court.)

———— Opowieści dziewczęce. (Girls' tales.)
Girls' letters representative of various periods in Polish history.

———— Przypadki krola jegomosci. (Adventures of his majesty the king.)
Story of the 18th century and King Joseph Poniatowski.

———— Sprawy ponure. (Melancholy circumstances.)
These stories bring in all Polish customs, and are most delightfully written. All works of this author are recommended.

*****Weyssenhof, Jozef.** Gromada. (The community.)

*———— Hetmani. (Commanders-in-chief.)

*———— Puszcza. (Wilderness.)

———— Sobòl i panna. (The sable and the girl.)

——— Sprawa Dołęgi. (The affair of Mr. Dolega.)

——— Zwycięzca. (The victor.)

A very good writer, the best being stories of country life in the Polish families of Lithuania.

*Żeromski, Stefan. Popioły. (Ashes.)

Historical novel of the period of 1796 and following. The story involves the wars of Napoleon in Russia and the Polish sympathy with Napoleon.

——— Ludzie bezdomni. (A homeless people.)

This is a book of great importance in Polish literature and in the history of Polish thought. The homeless people are exiles and patriots who sacrifice home to work for others.

——— Syzyfowe prace. (The labors of Sysyphus.)

——— Wiatr od morza. (The wind from the sea.)

His latest work, celebrating the Pole's love for the Baltic, access to which is now regained.

——— Wierna rzeka. (The faithful river.)

Time of the insurrection of 1863; a charming tale.

A literary craftsman of the first quality: some of his books ought to be in every collection, but must be chosen with discrimination, as his work includes titles which would have to be restricted according to American standards.

Żmijewska, Eugenia. Dola. (Fate.)

——— Płonyk. (A flame.)

——— Wbrew.

——— Żona. (The wife.)

Żuławski, Jerzy. Na srebrym globie. (On the silver globe.)

A colony from this world escaping to the moon finds there the descendants of a previous settlement, degenerate and dwarfed, but ready to fight to protect their possession of the silver globe.

——— Stara ziemia. (The old earth.)

Some of these moon dwellers come down to observe the earth. The Polish Jules Verne.

Language

Berger, Hugo. Łatwa metoda gruntownego mauczenia się w krótkiem czasie jezyka angielskiego. (Easy method of learning the English tongue.)

Not very good, but the best available.

Burt's. Polish-English dictionary. N. Y. A. L. Burt Co.

A good practical dictionary costing $1.00; that by Chodzko is fuller and costs $5.00.

Song Books

Konopnicka, Marya. Spiewnik dla dzieci. (Songbook for children.)

Baranski, Franciszek. Jeszcze Polska nie zginęła; pieśni patryotyczne i narodowe.

Patriotic songs, the title being that of the national hymn.

Biography

Chołoniewski, Antoni. Tadeusz Kościuszko.

The best life of Kościuszko for general use. That by Korzon is more scholarly.

Podbielski, Bronislaus. Wieniec liliowy. (A wreath of lilies.)

Lives of the saints.

Skarga, Piotr. Żywoty świętych. (Lives of the saints.)

Szajnocha, Karol. O królach i bohaterach.

Biographies of kings and heroes.

Tarnowski, Stanisłav. Adam Mickiewicz.

The greatest of Polish poets.

Witkiewicz, Stanisław. Matejko.

Matejko is considered the greatest artist of Poland.

Wojciechowski, Konstanty. Piotr Skarga.
Life of Skarga, a great prophet and priest.

Domestic Science

Kucharka polska i amerykánska. (Cook book.)

Metropolitan Life Insurance Co. Dziecko. (The child.)
Pamphlet free.

Griel, C. L. Dziecko. New York, Y.W.C.A. International Translation and Service Bureau. 1920. 47 p.

United States History, Civics, etc.

Dyniewicz, Władysław, pub. Historya Stanów Zjednoczonych. (History of the United States.) Chicago, 1886. 474 p.

Falkenhorst, Karl. Z dziejów odkrycia Ameryki. (American history.) Warsaw, Gebethner & Wolf. 1907. 506 p.

National Catholic Welfare Council. Civics catechism— English-Polish edition. (Parallel texts. An excellent work.) 1312 Massachusetts Ave., Washington, D. C. 1920. 100 p.

Pecorini, Alberto. Historya Ameriki. (Parallel text, Polish and English.) Published by Marshall Jones, 1923, under the auspices of the Massachusetts Society of Colonial Dames.

Sawicki, Jozef. Trésciwa historya Stanow Zjednoczonych. (Brief history of the United States.) Toledo, Paryski, 1910. 472 p.

Y. W. C. A. International Translation and Service Bureau. Poczatkowe szkolki dla dzieci. (The kindergarten.) 16 p.

—— Miedzynarodowy instytut dla kobiet i dziewa-zat. (The International Institute for women and girls.)

—— Sady oraz zastosowanie ustaw. (Courts of law and their use.) 13 p.

—— Co Ameryka ma dla was. (What America has for you.) 53 p.

Polish History

Lewicki, Anatol. Zarys historji polskiej. (Short history of Poland.)

Limanowski, B. Historya powstania narodu Polskiego. (History of the insurrections of Poland—19th century.)

Śliwiński, L. Jan Chodkiewicz.

—— Powstanie Listopadie.

—— Powstanie Kościuszkówskie.
A writer of great talent who makes history read like romance.

Travel

Dzieduszycka, E. H. Indye i Himalaje. (Travel in India and the Himalayas.)

Ossendowski, Ferdinand. Przez kraj, ludzi, zwierzat, i bogów. (Beasts, men and gods.)

Sienkiewicz, Henryk. Listy z Afriki. (Letters from Africa.)
Highly regarded and greatly enjoyed by Polish readers.

Literature

Asnyk, Adam. Poezye. (Poetry.)

Konopnicka, Marja. Poezye, 6 volumes.

Korzeniowski. Dzieła. (Works.)
A great dramatist; the father of Joseph Conrad.

Kwiaty i kłosy.
Collection of miscellaneous poems; suitable for recitation.

Mickiewicz, Adam. Pisma, 6 volumes.
If the whole set cannot be afforded, the single volume entitled Poezye (Poetry) is suggested.

Słowacki, Juliusz. Pisma. (Works.) 4 volumes.

Wyspiański, Stanisław. Wesele. (The wedding.)
A drama of distinction reproducing some historical scenes, a great favorite.

Czarkowski, Ludwik. Pseudonimy i kryptonimy polskie.
A useful index to the many pseudonyms used by Polish writers.

Translations from Other Literatures

Alcott, L. M. U progu życia. (Jo's boys.)

Amicis, E. de. Serce. (Heart of a boy—Cuore.)

Andersen, H. C. Baśnie i powiąski. (Fairy tales.)

Benson, R. H. Światło niewidzialne. (The light invisible.)

Bulwer-Lytton, E. G. E. Ostatnie dnie Pompei. (Last days of Pompeii.)

Burnett, F. H. Mały lord. (Little Lord Fauntleroy.)

Carroll, Lewis (pseud). Przygody Alinki w krainie czarow. (Alice in wonderland.)

Cervantes Saavedra, M. de. Don Kiszot z Manszy. (Don Quixote.)

Clemens, S. L. Humoreski. (Humorous selections.)

Conrad, Joseph. Fantazja Almayera. (Almayer's folly.)

Cooper, J. F. Progromca zwierza i ostatni Mohikanin. (Last of the Mohicans.)

—— Pionierowie. (Pioneers.)

Dante, Alighieri. Boska komedja. (Divine comedy.)

De Foe, Daniel. Robinson Kruzoe.

Dickens, Charles. David Copperfield.

—— Dombi i syn.

—— Klub Pickwicka.

—— O dwóch miastach. (Tale of two cities.)

Doyle, A. C. Czerwonym szlakiem. (A study in scarlet.)

—— Pamiętnik Holmesa. (Memoirs of Sherlock Holmes.)

——Pies Baskerville'ów. (Hound of the Baskervilles.)

—— Przygody Brygadyera Gerarda. (Adventures of Brigadier Gerard.)

—— Przygody Sherlocka Holmesa. (Adventures of Sherlock Holmes.)

Franklin, Benjamin. Pamiętniki. (Autobiography.)

Goethe, J. W. von. Faust.

Goldsmith, Oliver. Pleban z Wakefieldu. (Vicar of Wakefield.)

Grimm, J. & W. K. Baśnie. (Fairy tales.)

Hagenbeck, K. Z życia zwierzat w niewoli. (Training wild animals.)

Hamsun, Knut. Głód. (Hunger.)

Homer. Ilyada. (Iliad.)

—— Odysseja. (Odyssey.)

Hugo, Victor. Człowiek smiechu. (Man who laughs.)

—— Katedra N. M. P. (Notre Dame.)

—— Nędzarze. (Les Misérables.)

—— Pracownicy morza. (Toilers of the sea.)

—— Rok dziewięćdziesiąty trzeci. (Ninety-three.)

Ibsen, Henrik. Nora czyli dom lalki. (Doll's house.)

Keller, Helen. Historya mego życia. (Story of my life.)

Kipling, Rudyard. Kim.

—— Kzięga puszczy. (Jungle book.)

———— Druga księga puszczy. (Second jungle book.)

———— Stalky i sp.

———— Takie sobie bajeczki. (Just so stories.)

Lagerlöf, Selma. Tatniące serca.

Lamb, Charles. Powięsci Szekspira. (Tales from Shakespeare.)

London, Jack. Przygody psa w Klondyke. (Call of the wild.)

———— Żelazna stopa. (The iron heel.)

Loti, Pierre. Rybak islandzki. (Iceland fisherman.)

Maeterlinck, Maurice. Niebieski ptak. (Blue bird.)

Marryatt, Frederic. Warod koralowych raf. (Masterman Ready.)

Molière. Dzieła. (Works, translated by T. Żelenski.)

Montgomery, L. M. Ania z żielonego wzgorza. (Anne of Green Gables.)

Nansen, Fridtjof. Wśród nocy i lodów. (Farthest north.)

Poe, E. A. Morderstwo na Rue-Morgue. (Murders in the Rue Morgue.)

———— Opowieści nadzwyczajne. (Tales.)

Powieści z tysiąca i jednej nocy. (Arabian nights.)

Ruskin, John. Król złotej rzeki. (King of the golden river.)

Schiller, F. von. Dziewica Orleanska. (Maid of Orleans.)

Scott, Sir Walter. Czarny karżel. (Black dwarf.)

———— Iwanhoe.

———— Kenilworth.

———— Klasztor. (The monastery.)

———— Kwentyn Durward.

———— Lucya z Lamermoorn.

Shakespeare, Wm. Dzieła, 12 v. (Works.)

Smiles, Samuel. O charakterze. (Character.)

———— Pomoc własna. (Self-help.)

Stevenson, R. L. Dziwna historya Dr-a Jekyll'a i Mr-a Hyde'a. (Dr. Jekyll and Mr. Hyde.)

———— Skarby na wyspie. (Treasure island.)

Stowe, H. B. Chata wuja Toma. (Uncle Tom's Cabin.)

Swift, J. Podróże Guliwera. (Gulliver's travels.)

Thompson, Ernest Seton. Strzepouch matka liszka. (Biography of a silver fox.)

Tolstoi, L. N. Anna Karenina.

———— Wojna i pokój. (War and peace.)

Van Norman, Louis E. Polska jako rycerz wśród narodów. (Poland, the knight among nations.)

Wallace, Lew. Ben-Hur.

Washington, B. T. Autobiografia murzajna. (Up from slavery.)

Wilkins, M. E. Pembroke.

Wirgiljusz, P. Eneida. (Virgil's Eneid.)

Wiseman, N. P. S. Fabiola.

Printed in the USA
CPSIA information can be obtained
at www.ICGtesting.com
CBHW072151111224
18868CB00003B/47

9 781020 806216